1-DAY TRIPS FROM BENGALURU

This volume includes 1-day trips from Bengaluru to Devarayanadurga, Ghati Subramanya, Kotilingeshwara, Hogenakkal, Lepakshi, Bhoga Nandishwara, and Chikkaballapura.

Partha Majumdar

1

Copyright © 2023 Partha Majumdar

All rights reserved.

No part of this book may be reproduced, stored in a retrieval system, or transmitted in any form or by any means, electronic, mechanical, photocopying, recording, or otherwise, without express written permission of the publisher.

ISBN-13: 9798865142751

Cover design by Partha Majumdar

3

Preface

Since our return from Cyprus in November 2001, there were very few occasions when I lived at our home. This was because Deepshree restarted her career in Bengaluru, and I worked in Kolkata. Then, I lived alone in Saudi Arabia for work. During this period, we met about once every quarter.

In November 2013, I quit my job in Saudi Arabia to be able to live at our home. I set up a business in Bengaluru. It was a new adventure. However, we were all happy.

My next stint away from our home started in 2019. Between November 2013 and May 2019, we undertook many trips from Bengaluru. Generally, we traveled once every month.

This book chronicles our trips around Bengaluru, which we completed within a day.

On omission in this book are trips to Mysuru. Travel Agencies operate 1-day trips to Mysuru from Bengaluru. However, all our trips to Mysuru have been for at least two days.

5

Table of Contents

PREFACE 4

DEVARAYANADURGA 8

GHATI SUBRAMANYA 32

SHREE KOTILINGESHWARA 42

LEPAKSHI 62

HOGENAKKAL 78

SRI BHOGA NANDISHWARA 98

ISHA FOUNDATION, CHIKKABALLAPURA 106

NANDI HILLS 110

ABOUT THE AUTHOR 112

BOOKS IN THIS SERIES 114

OTHER BOOKS BY THE AUTHOR 118

7

Devarayanadurga

On 17th June 2018 (Sunday), at around 10 a.m., I saw a post on Facebook of one of my friends checking into Devarayanadurga. I had never heard of this place. The map in the post suggested that the place was close to Bengaluru. So, I checked the route map on Google Maps and found that the place was about 80 km from our house in Bengaluru.

At 10:30 a.m., I proposed to Deepshree that we visit this place. In turn, Deepshree asked Ranoo. Ranoo declined as she had to prepare for her Viva the next day. Luckily for me, Deepshree agreed to come along.

Devarayanadurga means "Fortress of the Gods."

"Durga" in Kannada means "Fort."

The Lords are referred to as "Devas."

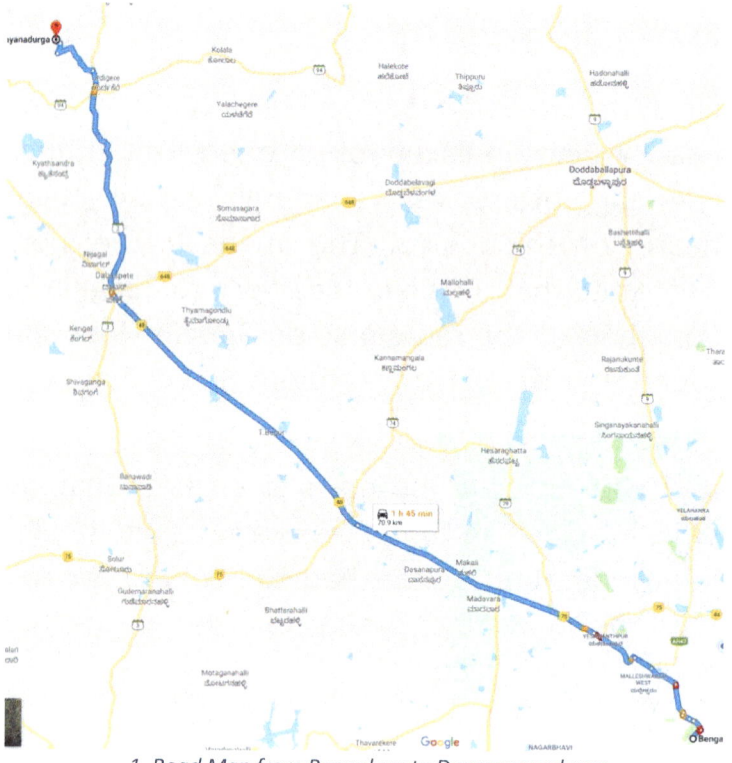

. 1. Road Map from Bengaluru to Devarayanadurga

We requested Ranoo to have lunch in a hotel close to our house, and she agreed. By Noon, we were ready. We decided to take our Innova.

. 2. Our Toyota Innova is ready for the drive.

First, we went to the Petrol Pump where we generally fill Diesel. We did not need Diesel that day as the tank was full. However, we got the tyres inflated. And we were ready.

We took the Outer Ring Road through Hebbal and BEL Circle to reach Gurugantapalya. From there, we took the highway. The roads were empty as this was the day after the Eid holiday and a Sunday. We soon reached the first Toll Gate. We paid Rs. 30 for a two-way pass.

Once through the Toll Gate, we were cruising at about 100 kmph. Soon, we reached the next Toll

Gate at Neelamangala. Here, we encountered many trunks lined up at the Toll Gate. We paid Rs. 36 for a two-way pass.

. 3. Massive number of Trucks at the Neelamangala Toll Gate.

Once we passed the Toll Gate, we were cruising at about 80 kmph. However, the large number of Trucks on the road meant that I had to be extremely careful while driving. The problem is that though there are signs all along the highway that the slow-moving vehicles must drive on the left lane, the Trucks always go on the inner lane. This highway has two lanes in each direction. In the outer lane, quite a few two-wheelers ply.

Soon, we realized we needed to take a diversion to the right from the highway. However, Deepshree was late in letting me know this. So, I overshot the diversion at Dabarspet and drove above the flyover. This place is confusing. However, an indicator is a Café Coffee Day on the other side of the flyover. This is the first Café Coffee Day on the highway till this point. It took us a drive of 5 km before we found a U-turn.

We took the U-turn and soon reached the intersection by driving on the service road. This time, we took the correct turn at the intersection and were on a good road. This road was a single road. We hardly found any traffic on this road. Also, the road was very well maintained. Soon, we saw road signs indicating we were going to Devarayanadurga.

. 4. 15 km from Devarayanadurga.

There is significantly less population around this road. There are vast fields on both sides of the road. All along, I found road signs with village names. However, these must be small villages.

Driving further, we soon found ourselves at the gates of Devarayanadurga. We took a diversion to the left to enter Devarayanadurga. It was 2:30 p.m. at that time.

. 5. Gates of Devarayanadurga.

From this point, we drove for another 5 km. On both sides, we found a thick forest. Also, we were gradually climbing. The road here is relatively narrow. So, when another car comes from the other side, it needs cautious driving.

We soon found ourselves at the checkpoint. Here, we needed to pay Rs. 20 for entering the premises. The Guard told us there were two temples in the premises – one next to the checkpoint and another on top of the hill.

We first went to the temple adjoining the checkpoint. There is a gate for this temple.

. 6. Gates of Devarayanadurga Temple 1.

We parked our vehicle just after entering the Gate. There is no formal parking place here. So, we parked at the edge of the road. We removed our slippers and kept them in the car. Then, we walked to the Temple premises.

Outside the Temple, there is a place to wash hands and feet. I washed my hands and feet. Then we entered the Temple. Incidentally, there was no network coverage from Airtel in this area.

We bought tickets for Rs. 20 (Rs. 10 * 2) for offering prayers. There are two temples on this premises – one is the Temple of Lord Narahimsa Swamy, and another is the Temple of Goddess

Lakshmi. We offered prayers in both temples. Inside the temple, we offered Dakshina of Rs. 30 in total.

. 7. The Lakshmi Temple in the premises. Goddess Lakshmi is the goddess of wealth. She is the wife of Lord Vishnu.

Lord Brahma is the creator, Lord Vishnu is the preserver, and Lord Shiva is the destroyer.

Photography was prohibited inside the temple where the idol of the deities is placed. This is generally the case in any Indian temple. We buy the photographs of the idols of the deities from the authorized stores on the temple premises. These stalls typically also have books with details of the temple.

8. The Narasimha Swamy Temple in the premises. The "Narasimha" is an incarnation of Lord Vishnu. He appears as half-man, half-lion. "Nara" means "Man," and "Simha" means "Lion."

. 9. Deepshree with the Prasad.

On coming out of the Temple, we found one family was serving prasad to all the people. We also took prasad consisting of Dal, Cucumber, Coconut mix (called "**Kosambri**" in Karnataka), and Butter Milk (Curd mixed with Water and Salt).

We spent some more time at the premises and took some pictures.

. 10. The Entrance to the Temple Premises. In every temple in South India, one will find an elaborate structure at the entrance.

. 11. Sculptures at the Entrance of the Temple. On the left top, one can see an idol of Lord Ganesha.

We left the Temple Premises and were back in our car. We noticed that there is a Toilet just outside the premises. It is a Free Toilet. We discovered that it is in a decent state, though not great.

. 12. Toilet at the Temple Premises.

From this point, we could see the hill we had to climb to reach the other Temple Premises.

. 13. Hills in the surrounding.

We started the climb. The road is narrow. And several vehicles were climbing down. So, I had to be very careful. The drive took about 25 minutes. Soon, we were at the top of the hill till the point where there was a drivable road.

We found that there were a lot of cars here. The regular parking place was packed. So, we parked the car at the side of the road. We found a place where there were only two cars. I decided to turn the vehicle before parking. This proved to be a good decision as this place also got full by the time we were ready to leave this place.

. 14. Near where we parked our car.

After parking the vehicle, we started towards the Temple premises. We discovered that the Temple was further up. So, we started climbing up the stairs.

. 15. Stairs in the Temple Premises.

The stairs are wide and thus not very difficult to climb. However, there are about 175 steps to climb before reaching the top. There are some shops on the way selling snacks.

. 16. Gate along the way.

The view is beautiful from the top.

. 17. View of the valley.

We kept climbing further. The stairs did not seem to end. After climbing quite a few steps, we found a Hanuman Temple.

. 18. Hanuman Temple in Devarayanadurga.

On reaching the top, we left our slippers in the place appointed for the same. There is a caretaker to take care of the slippers.

We entered the Temple premises. Two boys were sitting at the gate. They put tika on our heads. And then they demanded money. So, I paid them Rs. 20.

We entered the Temple premises. The main temple is that of Narasimha Swamy. We offered our prayers. Then, we came out of the temple premises.

Outside the Temple Premises, there is a small pond.

. 19. Pond in the Temple premises.

As I was taking photos of the pond and the surroundings, I got disconnected from Deepshree. On returning, I could not find her anywhere. I tried calling her and found that there was no network. I waited for 20 minutes where we had left our slippers. Then I thought that she must have climbed down.

So, I collected both slippers, paid the caretaker, put on my slippers, held Deepshree's slippers in my hand, and started climbing down, looking for Deepshree. I found her nowhere till I reached the end of the stairs. So, I waited there.

Suddenly, I got a call, and it was Deepshree's. She told me that she was still at the top. So, I told her to climb down. Soon, we were reunited.

By this time, we were starving. So, we bought some pakodas. This is what was available here.

. 20. Food stalls at the Temple Premises. It is better to carry some food while visiting Devarayanadurga.

After having the pakodas, we boarded our car. It was 4:00 p.m. at this time. There was a thick cloud gathering at this point. So, we decided to hurry.

This Temple is open between 10:00 a.m. and 5:30 p.m.

. 21. Thick clouds over Devarayanadurga.

Soon, we were climbing down the hill. We passed the checkpoint and were on our way back.

While coming to the Temple, I noticed a big lake. So, I went searching for the same on the way back. Soon, we were at the spot.

This is a lovely spot with a vast lake and a beach. Lots of people were enjoying the water. This place is a perfect Picnic Spot.

. 22. A Picnic Spot in Devarayanadurga.

We were soon out of the gate and returning to Bengaluru. We had a pleasant drive till we reached the highway. On the way, we bought half a Jackfruit for Rs. 100.

On reaching the highway, we found massive traffic on the road. There were a lot of huge trucks. So, I had to drive very carefully. We crossed three accident sites on the way till we reached Gurugantapalya. Soon, we took the road towards our house in RT Nagar. On reaching CBI Road, we decided to stop at Brahmin's Idly to have Thatte Idly. Both of us were very hungry. We had 2 Idlies each and Coffee for Rs. 92.

We returned home by 7:20 p.m., in time for the Germany versus Mexico match.

Ghati Subramanya

15 August 2018 was Nag Panchami. Deepshree had planned to offer Puja at home on that day. As it was also Independence Day, everyone at home had a holiday. We had contacted our Purohit, Pandit Ravi Sharma, and he had agreed to conduct the Puja. He told us that he would start the Puja at 5:00 a.m. So, we all got up by 4:00 a.m. and got ready. However, the Puja started at around 6:30 a.m.

> 15th August is India's Independence Day and is thus a Public Holiday in India.

> "Nag" refers to snakes, specifically cobras.
>
> The creator deity Brahma relegated the Nagas to the nether regions when they became too populous on earth and commanded them to bite only the truly evil or those destined to die prematurely. They are also associated with waters - rivers, lakes, seas, and wells - and are guardians of treasure.
>
> Source: https://www.britannica.com/topic/naga-Hindu-mythology

> According to Hindu mythology, Kaliya Nag created havoc and was killing humans. Lord Krishna defeated Kaliya Nag and got Kaliya Nag's commitment not to disturb humans.
>
> The day of the victory of Lord Krishna over Kaliya Nag is celebrated as Nag Panchami.
>
> Lord Krishna is an incarnation of Lord Vishnu, the preserver.

The Puja took about 2 hours. At the end of the Puja, Pandit Ravi Sharma told us there was a vast Subramanya Swami temple nearby at Ghati Subramanya.

> For the Hindus, Lord Brahma is the creator, Lord Vishnu is the preserver, and Lord Shiva is the destroyer. Lord Shiva is married to Goddess Parvati. The children of Lord Shiva and Goddess Parvati are Lord Ganesha, Lord Kartekeya, Goddess Lakshmi, and Goddess Saraswati.

> In South India, Lord Kartekeya is known as Lord Subramanya.
>
> According to Hindu mythology, Lord Kartekeya defeated the Nagas. So, any Hindu seeking protection from the Nagas, pray to Lord Subramanya.

Immediately, we planned that we would go there the same day. I checked Google Maps and found the route. We had to drive through Doddaballapura. We had been to Doddaballapura earlier. We were initially considering buying a plot of land close to Doddaballapura.

After the Puja, we had breakfast. Riya decided to go with Ujwala and Bhavitha to Orion Mall as she had to buy some essentials. So, that left Ranoo, Deepshree, and me for the Ghati Subramanya trip. We started from our house at around 11:00 a.m.

We first visited the Subramanya Swami temple close to our house in Kaval Byra Sandra. We offered our prayers. Here, we met the Treasurer of the Temple. He started explaining the various plans he had for the Temple. We committed to donating Rs. 20,000 for the new construction.

At around 12:30 p.m., we started for Ghati Subramanya. We drove past CBI Road to get onto the Airport Road. From there, we took the service road to get into Yelahanka. From Yelahanka, we took the road to Doddaballapura.

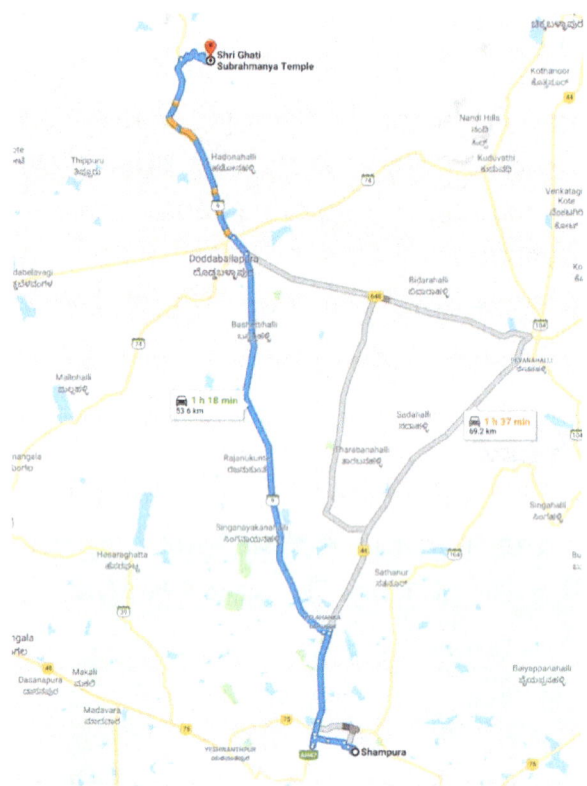

. 23. Road Map from Bengaluru to Ghati Subramanya.

The road to Doddaballapura is good. However, there is a fair stretch that is under construction. So, only one side of the road is open. We reached Doddaballapura at around 1:30 p.m.

At Doddaballapura, they are making a flyover over the Railway Lines. So, we had to take the old road, which is extremely tricky. We crossed that and were on the other side. Driving a little bit more, we were at Shree Ganesh Grand. We decided to have lunch here.

. 24. Hotel Sri Ganesh Grand, Doddaballapura.

The toilets at Hotel Ganesh Grand are pretty good. On the 1st floor, there is an air-conditioned restaurant. We ordered South Indian Deluxe Thali for each of us. At around 2:30 p.m., we once again started for Ghati Subramanya. I noticed that we were about 29 km away.

The road is pretty good. There was one confusing point where we had to decide to take a right turn on a bridge, and we did that correctly. Driving a bit more, we found a side road with a board for Ghati Subramanya. We took that diversion. Soon, we were going on a single road. There were a fair number of cars on the road. So, we had to drive slowly. We crossed a Railway Gate on the way.

Then, we came across a traffic jam. The villagers had set up a temporary market, and many people were buying from them. It took nearly 30 minutes to get through this. Driving another 5 km, we were at Ghati Subramanya.

We parked our car at a distance in the open field. Some villagers were taking care of the vehicles. Our decision was good as the Temple's Parking place was packed. We walked to the Temple.

> Usually, Subramanya Swami Temples are on top of a hill. However, Ghati Subramanya Temple is in a valley. "Ghati" means Valley.

Outside the Temple, there are a lot of Stones with Nagas.

. 25. Outside the Ghati Subramanya Temple.

We bought offerings from a Lady and left our slippers at her stall. We walked to the main Temple.

. 26. Entrance to the Main Temple.

There was a massive rush at the Temple as it was Nag Panchami. We were lucky as about 10 minutes after our entry, they stopped anyone from entering the temple. We walked the pile of people to reach the ticket counter. We had to buy tickets for Rs. 50 per person.

Once we entered the Temple, we had to walk along the guided path. It took us nearly 2 hours in this line to reach the deity. It was a very tiring experience. When we got the deity, we had about 5 seconds to offer our prayers and were pushed out.

We came out of the Temple, collected our slippers, and were back in our car. We gave Rs. 20 to the villagers for looking after the car. Then, we drove back to our home in Bengaluru.

Shree Kotilingeshwara

Baba came to visit us for two weeks. We were overjoyed. However, the day he arrived, I received an intimation from Thailand to submit our response to an RFP. This was also excellent news. We were awaiting this intimation for the last five months. However, this meant that I would have very little time for Baba. Baba understood this and encouraged me to concentrate on the RFP.

I had time till 9 September 2018 to submit our response. So, I decided we would go out somewhere with Baba on one of the two Sundays he was here. Taking a break on 9 September 2018 would be very risky. So, we decided to use 2 September 2018 to visit Kotilingeshwara.

I discovered that Shree Kotilingeshwara Temple was about 95 km from our house. So, it was feasible to go and come back the same day. We planned to start at 7:30 a.m. However, we could only start by 8:30 a.m. Fortunately, as it was Sunday, we did not face any traffic till we reached KR Puram. Usually, there is massive traffic at KR Puram. We did not meet any traffic at KR Puram and were quickly driving on the KR Puram bridge on the Kolar Road.

. 27. Road Map - Bengaluru to Shree Kotilingeshwara Temple.

After crossing KR Puram Bridge, we faced a little traffic near the crossing to Hoodi junction. After that, the road was empty. We drove on at about 100 kmph. We came across one Toll Gate. We had to pay Rs. 25 for a 2-way day pass. There was a little rush at the Toll Gate.

. 28. Toll Gate at Hoskote.

At around 9:30 a.m., we were crossing Hoskote. Soon, I found a notice board for a Restaurant. I parked our car to find ourselves at Nandi Grand.

. 29. Hotel Nandi Grand, Hoskote.

There is a small Hanuman Temple at the Entrance of Nandi Grand.

. 30. Hanuman Temple at Hotel Nandi Grand. Lord Hanuman was the son of Anjana and is thus also called Lord Anjaneya.

At Nandi Grand, we found that they were having a Dosa festival. There was a separate menu for the different types of Dosas they served. They also displayed samples of each type of Dosa.

31. Display of different types of Dosas in Hotel Nandi Grand.

There are two sections at Nandi Grand. Outside is a self-service section, and there is an air-conditioned hall where they provide service. We decided to go to the Air-Conditioned Hall. It was full. However, we got a table with six seats. Riya,

Baba, and I ordered Dosa. Riya and I also ordered a Dahi Vada (Vada dipped in Curd) each. Deepshree ordered Rava Idli and Dahi Vada.

. 32. Breakfast at Hotel Nandi Grand.

We ordered Sagoo Dosa. I enjoyed the Dosa. It filled my stomach. So, I decided to skip the Dahi Vada. Baba came to the rescue as he had the Dahi Vada. Immediately, he declared that he would not have lunch.

. 33. Deepshree with the Rava Idli.

There is a clean restroom at Nandi Grand. We all refreshed ourselves, unsure of what we would find during the rest of the trip. Deepshree and Riya went around clicking snaps at Nandi Grand.

At around 10:30 a.m., we started from Nandi Grand, having spent around an hour here. Suddenly, it struck us that the Temple may close for the afternoon. So, we made a target to reach Shree Kotilingeshwara Temple by Noon. We checked Google Maps, which stated we would reach by 12:35 p.m.

I was driving at 100-120 kmph as the road was empty. It was an excellent road till we reached Kolar.

. 34. Road to Kolar. Kolar is a town in Karnataka, India, with a Gold Mine. However, no gold can be found here now.

Enroute to Kolar.

After crossing Kolar, we had to take a diversion off the highway. Soon, we found ourselves on a single road. I could drive at around 50 kmph. Google Maps suggested we had to drive about 30 km this way. There was a small patch of about 5 km where the road was under construction. This meant that we had to drive on mud roads here.

. 35. There is an enormous lake in Kolar on the way to *Shree Kotilingeshwara*.

After crossing this stretch, Google Maps suggested we were 5 km from the Shree

Kotilingeshwara Temple. We were now on a wider Main Road. We reached the Shree Kotilingeshwara Temple at 12:33 p.m.

To enter the Shree Kotilingeshwara Temple, we had to pay Rs. 50 as the Parking Fees. We found parking inside the Temple premises. This parking space is covered. However, there is a vast parking space outside the Temple. I don't know what the parking fees are here.

Right opposite the Parking Area is a Sathya Sai Baba Temple. We offered our prayers here. However, we hurried on, unsure if the main temple would close for lunch.

We found a small Lakshmi Temple as we proceeded to the Main Temple. We stopped there and offered our prayers.

36. Shree Lakshmi Temple at Shree Kotilingeshwara.

From the Lakshmi Temple, the entrance to the Shree Kotilingeshwara Temple is about 20 meters. At the Shree Kotilingeshwara Temple entrance, we had to buy tickets at Rs. 20 per head. Then, we had to follow a defined path. The moment we entered the Shree Kotilingeshwara Temple, we were overwhelmed by seeing so many Shiv Lings.

. 37. At the entrance of the Shree Kotilingeshwara Temple.

38. More Shiv Lings near the entrance of the Shree Kotilingeshwara Temple.

There are three Temples in the Shree Kotilingeshwara Temple complex. We went through them.

> The Pujari in one of the temples told us that this complex had around 90 Lakhs Shiv Lings. The target was to create one crore Shiv Lings. Thus, the name of this Temple was Kotilingeshwara.

> "Koti" means "a crore," and "Ling" refers to "Shiv Lings" dedicated to Lord Shiva or Mahadev.

After going through the three temples, we visited another part of the Shree Kotilingeshwara Temple. Here, there are some small temples.

Then, there is an open field with lakhs of Shiv Lings. There is a massive Shiv Ling in the center.

. 39. In the field where there are lakhs of Shiv Lings. Most of the Shiv Lings are donated. These Shiv Lings have the names of the donors. Also, all the Shiv Lings are numbered.

. 40. The huge Shiv Ling.

This complex has a huge Nandi and three slightly smaller Shiv Lings.

. 41. One of the three slightly smaller Shiv Lings.

. 42. Another of the three slightly smaller Shiv Lings.

. 43. The gigantic idol of Nandi ji in Swamy Kotilingeshwara. Nandi ji is the vahana of Lord Shiva. "Vahana" means "vehicle."

We bought the Laddoo Prasad. There are two varieties – one costs Rs. 50 each and another one costs Rs. 20 each.

After spending about 30 minutes here, we walked towards the exit. At the exit, there is an Idol of Lord Ganesha.

44. An idol of Lord Ganesha at the Swamy Kotilingeshwara Temple.

We came out of the Temple complex at around 3:15 p.m. There are restrooms near the Parking Area. However, these are not very clean.

We started back for Bengaluru at around 3:30 p.m. We drove back fast. We were near Nagawara at around 5:30 p.m. We stopped at Café Coffee Day opposite the Veterinary College because we had not had lunch. We had something to eat. We were back inside our house at around 6:30 p.m.

61

Lepakshi

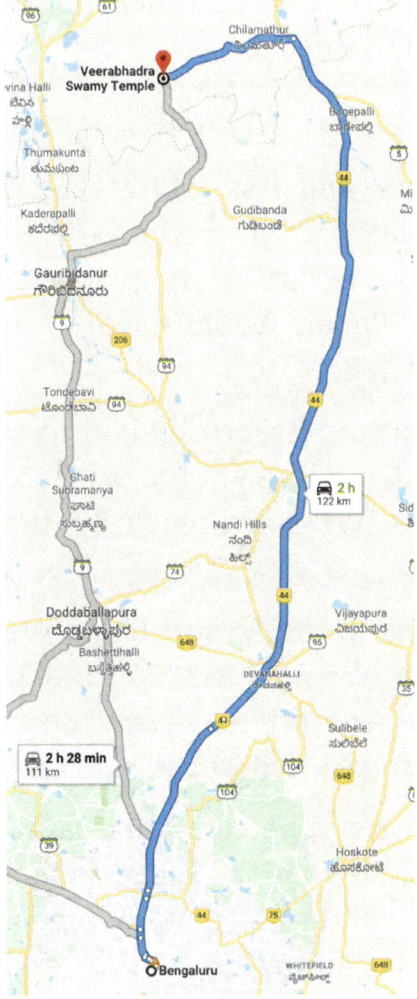

13-Jan-2019 was a Sunday. We planned for a short trip close to Bengaluru, which we could complete within the day. After a brief search, I found that the Lepakshi Temple was about 130 km from our house. So, we could reach there in about 2 hours. I searched Google Maps and found the route to the Lepakshi Temple. The Lepakshi Temple is also called the Veerabhadra Swamy Temple.

45. Route Map from Bengaluru to the Lepakshi Temple.

> In Ramayana, Lepakshi is where Jatayu fought with Ravana when Ravana was carrying Mata Sita to Lanka.

Maa, Riya, Deepshree, and I started at about 9:30 a.m. Ranoo stayed back in the house with Sheru and Baghira as she had to complete her college assignments. Ranoo would have lunch with Ujwala and Bhavitha.

We drove our Innova to the Petrol Pump near our house and filled diesel. We got the pressure checked on the tyres. We were ready for the journey.

We were soon driving on the Airport Road. We reached the Toll Gate. We paid Rs. 130 for a 2-way journey. From here on, we were on a relatively empty Bengaluru-Hyderabad highway.

At about 10:30 a.m., we stopped at a hotel called "Singara Gardenia". We had a South Indian breakfast comprising Idly, Masala Dosa, Upma (called Khara Bath in Bengaluru), Vada, and Coffee. It tasted good, possibly because we all started without having anything.

. 46. We had breakfast at Singara Gardenia.

After breakfast, we started on our way at about 11:30 a.m. The Google Maps indicated that we would be at our destination in about an hour.

We drove along the highway. The traffic was relatively low. Significantly, very few heavy vehicles were on the way. The road is exceptionally well maintained. There are small hills along the road. These hills look spectacular.

. 47. View from our car on the way to Lepakshi.

We kept driving on the highway till we reached a place called Kodikonda. Here, we had to get off the highway and turn left. An indicator on the highway indicates that Lepakshi is on the left. There is a gate here with a statue of a bird.

Here, there was construction work in progress. They were widening the minor road into a 6-lane road. So, we plodded from here onwards. From this point, Lepakshi Temple is about 10 km away. However, as work on the road was progressing throughout this length, I had to drive at a very moderate speed. In addition, many houses are on both sides of the road, resulting in many people and animals crossing.

I was looking for a place to park our car when I reached the Temple premises. First, we came across the Jatayuvu Theme Park. We drove past it. This was a mistake.

We reached the marketplace within 100 meters. Then, we found an indicator for a left turn to the Temple Premises. I took this turn. Then, I had to drive through a narrow road with cars parked on the left and shops on the right. With cars coming from the front, it was tough to drive here.

With a lot of difficulty, with one car even banging onto the side of our car, we negotiated this stretch and found a place to park our car right in front of the temple.

We should have taken the left at the Jatayuvu Theme Park, as that road leads to the main parking area for the temple.

. 48. Entrance to the Lepakshi Temple.

. 49. On entering the Lepakshi Temple.

We had to climb stairs to enter the Temple's main building. Beautiful sculptures and idols of many Gods and Goddesses are inside this stone-walled building.

> The Temple is formed on a set of stone pillars. The Temple's main attraction is that one pillar does not rest on the floor. One can test this as a piece of cloth can be passed under the base of this pillar.
>
> This mystery has yet to be solved since the 16th century.

. 50. Sculptures inside the Lepakshi Temple. Each pillar has some exquisite sculptures.

68

. 51. The Hanging Pillar in the Lepakshi Temple.

We could not locate this pillar when we visited the Lepakshi Temple for the first time. We finally found this pillar on our third visit.

. 52. Navagraha inside the Lepakshi Temple.

. 53. Outside the main temple.

54. Around the Lepakshi Temple.

55. There is a massive Shiv Ling in the Temple Premises.

The artisans did not complete the temple. Many parts of the temple have incomplete structures.

. 56. One of the incomplete structures.

After leaving the Lepakshi Temple, we drove to the Jatayuvu Theme Park. It is about 100 meters from the Temple. There is an ample amount of parking space here. This park was under construction. However, there is an entry fee of Rs. 10 per person.

There is one hill inside the Jatayu Theme Park. At the top of the hill is a massive statue of Jatayu. While climbing this hill, there are several things to see.

57. Statue of Jatayu.

. 58. The Lepakshi temple premises are seen from the top of Jatayu Theme Park.

. 59. The village around the Lepakshi Temple.

We started back for Bengaluru from Jatayuvu Theme Park at around 2:30 p.m. We drove back the same way we had come here.

Now, we were looking for a place to have lunch. We kept driving till we were about 10 km away from Devanahalli. Here, we found a hotel named Fish Land. We stopped here to have lunch.

. 60. At the entrance of Hotel Fish Land.

After lunch, comprising Chicken Curry, Rice, and Mutton Biriyani, we started to Bengaluru. We reached home by about 6:00 p.m.

Hogenakkal

Hogenakkal Waterfalls is about 180 km from Bengaluru. It is in the state of Tamil Nadu. I found this out quite some time back. I had been planning a trip to Hogenakkal for more than a month. However, the plan materialized on 17 February 2019 (Sunday).

On Saturday, it was decided that Deepshree, Riya, and I would go to Hogenakkal. Maa said she did not want to spend so much time in the sun. Ranoo said that she must finish her assignments from her college. Late in the night, Deepshree roped in Ujwala and Bhavitha. Ujwala is my sister-in-law, and Bhavitha is Ujwala's daughter.

We decided that we would start by 7 a.m. However, by the time we could start, it was 8 a.m. We took our Innova, as there were 6 of us. Maa also joined us when we were getting ready in the morning. So, we were Deepshree, Riya, Maa, Ujwala, Bhavitha, and I on our way to Hogenakkal.

We first filled Diesel near our house and started our journey.

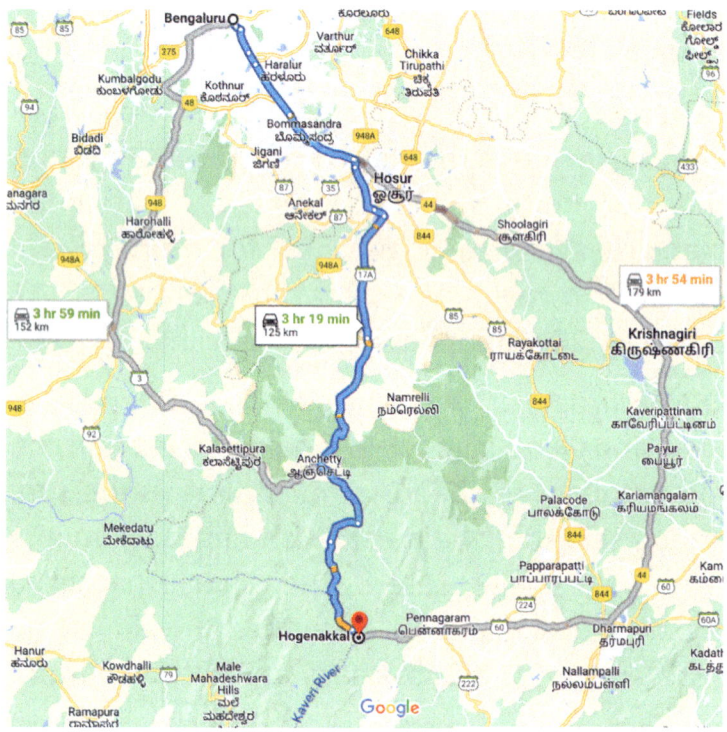

. 61. Road Map - Bengaluru to Hogenakkal. This route is through the Ghat section. The roads on this route are narrow and pass through a series of hills. So, there are a lot of sharp curves on this route.

Google Maps suggested we would reach Hogenakkal in about 3 hours. However, we took nearly 6 hours to reach Hogenakkal.

We drove down Hosur Road Flyover. We paid the toll of Rs. 70 for a 2-way pass. Then, I drove along to the Tamil Nadu-Karnataka border. Again, we paid a toll of Rs. 40 for a 2-way pass. Then we drove towards Hosur town.

The Google Map suggested we take a diversion to the right at Attibele. However, we missed it as there was a massive truck to our right.

We drove on, looking for a U-turn. However, we had to drive nearly 7 km before finding a U-turn. We went back to that junction. It was already about 10 a.m. at this time. So, we stopped at A2B for breakfast. We also had to take our Diabetes medicines.

. 62. A2B Restaurant in Hosur.

63. At A2B, Hosur.

We had Idli, Puri, Pongal, and Upma for breakfast. Bhavitha and Riya also had an Ice Cream.

After breakfast, we started on our way to Hogenakkal. This time, we took the turn at Attibele and were on track.

Now, we were driving on a single road. The road is just two lanes and with vehicles moving on both sides. As we passed through several villages, many people and cattle were on the road. So, we were plodding.

After driving for about an hour, we came to the Ghat section. Here, the road was through the hills. There were a lot of sharp turns on the way. So, I had to drive very carefully.

We were driving through the curvy roads in the Ghat section.

We drove for nearly one hour through the Ghat Section. Suddenly, we could see the Kaveri River. As we closed in, we saw some cars parked on the road and people on the banks of the river. So, we stopped our car and got down. We walked down to the banks of River Kaveri.

. 64. River Kaveri.

. 65. On the banks of River Kaveri.

This place is filthy. A lot of people were drinking alcohol and swimming in the river here. So, after a little while, we returned to the car and drove to Hogenakkal.

We reached a gate. Here, we had to pay Rs. 50 as parking fees. We were told that we were in Hogenakkal. We drove for another 15 minutes to reach the Hogenakkal Waterfalls.

We reached Hogenakkal at about 2 p.m.

We were looking for a place to park our car when one local told us to drive to Hotel Tamil Nadu, where we could find a parking place. So, we did that. We had to pay Rs. 50 for parking in Hotel Tamil Nadu.

. 66. Parking at Hotel Tamil Nadu.

After we parked our car, one person explained to Deepshree how to see the waterfall. We had to hire a "Tappa".

> "Tappa" is the boat used at Hogenakkal.

Each Tappa can carry four people. As there were 6 of us, we hired two Tappas. The guide showed us to the counter from where we had to buy the tickets for the Tappa. I paid Rs. 750 each for two Tappas.

. 67. The Ticket Counter for hiring Tappas.

Once we had paid for the Tappas, we had to wait to get our Life Jackets.

85

. 68. The Life Jacket Counter.

. 69. The Waiting Room at the Tappa Ghat.

Getting into the Tappa is challenging as it is precarious. Especially, Maa had a very tough time. Nevertheless, we managed.

. 70. Riya, Ujwala, and Bhavitha in one of the two Tappas.

. 71. The Tappa is in motion. The Pilot rows the Tappa with one oar.

The Tappa took us a little distance and asked us to get down. So, we got down from the Tappa. They asked us to walk along a path to where the Tappa would pick us up again.

. 72. The place where we got down from the Tappa.

. 73. The Pilot carries the Tappa to the next pick-up point. Each Tappa weighs about 50 Kgs.

We walked down about 150 meters to reach a spot where we had to board the Tappa again. Here, there were steep stairs. Maa had quite a difficulty getting down these stairs. However, we all managed.

. 74. Steep Stairs before getting on to the Tappa again.

Again, we boarded the Tappas. Ujwala, Riya, and Bhavitha were on one Tappa. Maa, Deepshree, and I were on the other Tappa.

The Tappa took us to the Hogenakkal Waterfall.

. 75. Hogenakkal Waterfall.

From the Waterfalls, our Tappas took us boating on the Kaveri River.

It is essential to carry one extra set of clothes. This is because the Trousers get completely wet sitting in the Tappa.

Our Tappa driver took us to where they were selling Fish Fry. These are fresh River Fish. I bought eight pieces for Rs. 200. They were delicious.

. 76. Eating Fresh Fish Fry.

The Tappa ride was for an hour. Again, we had to walk after the Tappa dropped us. Furthermore, the Tappa drivers carried the Tappas. We again boarded the Tappa to return to the Tappa boarding station.

I paid Rs. 250 each to the two Tappa drivers.

It was nearly 4 p.m. by the time we were back.

We were starving by now. So, we went to a Hotel near the Gate. We had Sambhar Rice. They also gave some Potato Fry and Pappad.

. 77. Waiting for lunch to arrive.

After lunch, we started on our way back home. It was nearly 5 p.m. when we started. So, I did not want to drive back the way we had come to Hogenakkal. This was because it would be going through the Ghat in the night. So, we took the much longer road through Dharmapuri.

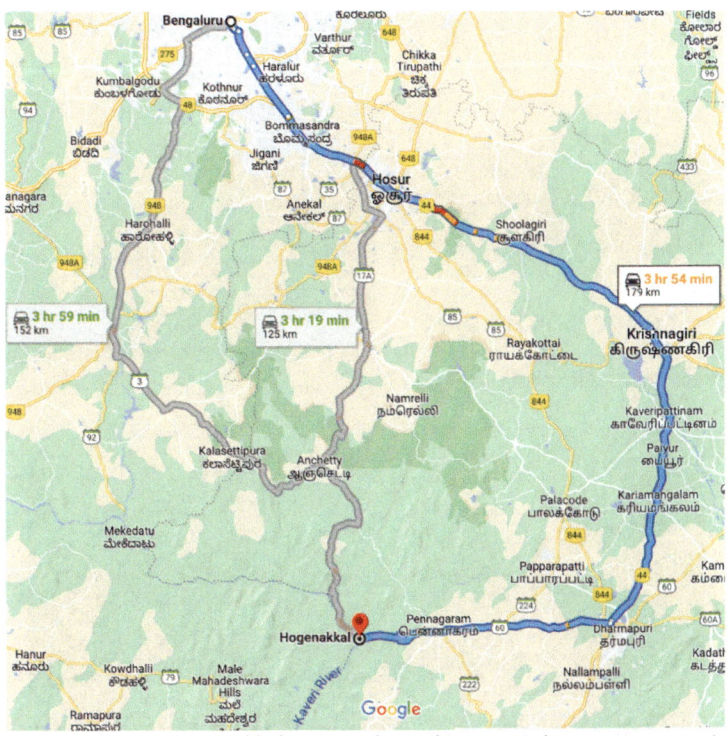

. 78. Road Map - Hogenakkal to Bengaluru. This route is longer. However, it takes less time as it is a highway.

My decision was excellent. We had to drive through the Ghat for about 35 km before we reached Dharmapuri. From Dharmapuri, we were on National Highway number 44, which is a 6-lane highway.

However, the highway was full of traffic. Also, there were a considerable number of heavy lorries on the road. I was driving at about 80 kmph but had to go carefully.

Scenes on the way back.

When we reached Dharmapuri, we wanted to have Tea. However, we could not find anything till we reached Krishnagiri town.

. 79. The Hotel where we had Tea at around 7:30 p.m.

This hotel is right after the Krishnagiri Toll Plaza. I paid Rs. 65 at this Toll Plaza for a one-way pass.

We drove back briskly and reached the Electronic City in Bengaluru. Then, we faced a massive traffic jam. We passed through the traffic jam and got home at 10:00 p.m. I ordered food from the Chinese Hotel next to our apartment. They delivered the food. We all took a bath, ate food, and slept.

Sri Bhoga Nandishwara

On the 14th of March 2021 (Sunday) morning, I read a Facebook post about a place near Bengaluru called Sri Bhoga Nandishwara in one of my groups. On checking Google Maps, I found that this place was about 50 km from our house. I proposed to Ranoo to visit Bhoga Nandishwara. She immediately agreed.

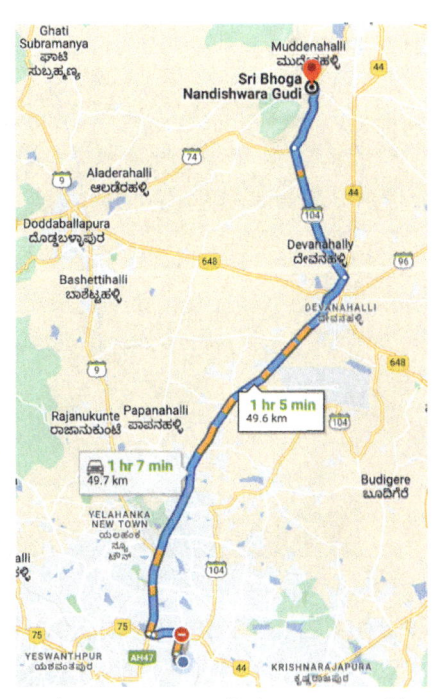

By noon, we were in our Ciaz headed to Bhoga Nandishwara. We took the CBI Road to reach the Airport Road. The road was relatively empty as it was a Sunday. We crossed the Toll Gate before the Airport and were soon in Devanahalli.

It was about 1 p.m., so we had lunch at Hotel Srinidhi Vaibhava. There is ample parking area at this hotel.

. 80. Hotel Srinidhi Vaibhava only serves vegetarian food.

We ordered a South Indian Thali each.

. 81. Ranoo with her South Indian Thali.

At around 2 p.m., we resumed our journey. For most of the way, we drove on the Bengaluru-Hyderabad highway.

. 82. On Bengaluru-Hyderabad highway near Devanahalli.

. 83. Scene along the Bengaluru-Hyderabad highway.

We took a diversion to our left. Here, we drove on a single road. This road is well maintained, though it passes through several villages. There are lots of vineyards on both sides of the roads.

. 84. One of the vineyards on the way to the Bhoga Nandishwara.

Soon, we reached our rendezvous. The Bhogi Nandishwara Temple is in a small village.

. 85. A hill near the Bhoga Nandishwara Temple.

Mahashivratri that year was celebrated on the 11th of March. The villagers organize a fair in the Bhoga Nandishwara Temple during this festival. This fair was still on when we visited. As a result, there were lots of people at the temple. Also, there were a lot of police officers in and around the temple complex.

> On Mahashivratri, Hindus offer prayers to Lord Shiva. The ritual on this day is to pour milk on Shiv Ling.

86. This structure is on the boundary walls of the Bhoga Nandishwara Temple, close to where we parked our car.

We entered the temple complex. There are no entry tickets. The temple complex is reasonably large, with three main buildings. We offered our prayers.

. 87. Pillars in the temple premises.

Bhoga Nandishwara is a beautiful temple. However, it could be better taken care of. Authorities like the Archeological Society of India (ASI) should take over the maintenance of the temple.

. 88. Pond in the temple premises.

After spending about 45 minutes in the temple, we returned to our car. We drove back home. On the way, we stopped at a Café Coffee Day. By 6:00 p.m., we were home.

Isha Foundation, Chikkaballapura

Chikkaballapura is a popular location for rock climbing close to Bengaluru. It is now becoming famous for a Shiva Temple developed by the Isha Foundation.

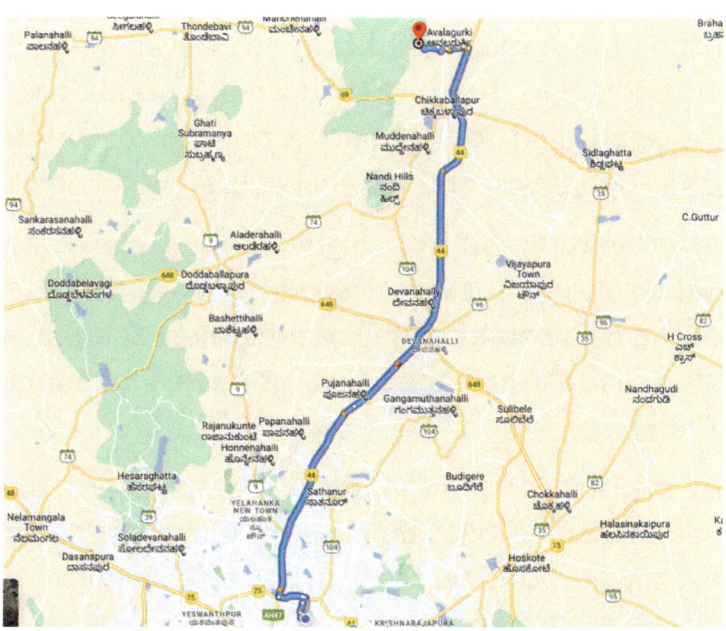

89. Road Map from Bengaluru to the Isha Foundation, Chikkaballapura. The Isha Foundation is about 70 km from Bengaluru off the Bengaluru-Hyderabad highway.

The main center of the Isha Foundation is at Coimbatore in Tamil Nadu. People visit the Isha

Foundation to practice yoga and meditation. The Isha Foundation has set up a new center in Chikkaballapura.

On 19 August 2023 (Sunday), I thought of visiting the Isha Foundation in Chikkaballapura. Deepshree has a working day on Sundays, so I drove to the Isha Foundations alone.

I took the Airport Road to reach Devanahalli at around 1 p.m. There I had lunch in a hotel. From Devanahalli, it took about an hour to reach the Isha Foundation at Chikkaballapura.

After getting off the highway, a single road passes through several villages to reach the gate of the Isha Foundation. From here on, there is a mud road through the hills. This drive is for about 7 km.

At the Isha Foundation, there is ample space for parking. Some villagers have set up shops selling food, water, and tea/coffee. The place is not very developed except for the foundation's center.

At the Isha Foundation, many volunteers guide the visitors through the facilities. Generally, some program is organized here. The day I visited, there was no program.

There are no entry fees here. I spent about 30 minutes at the center after offering my prayers. I bought Prasad for Rs. 200. Then, I returned home.

90. The statue of Adi Yogi at the Isha Foundation.

Nandi Hills

This book is incomplete without a mention of Nandi Hills. Nandi Hills is a popular picnic spot near Bengaluru. We have been to Nandi Hills many times. Reaching Nandi Hills from our house takes a little more than an hour. It is off the Bengaluru-Hyderabad highway.

Tipu Sultan used Nandi Hills as a summer retreat. So, there is a fort in Nandi Hills. The place has been developed to include hotels and needed public amenities. On the way, many resorts have been built.

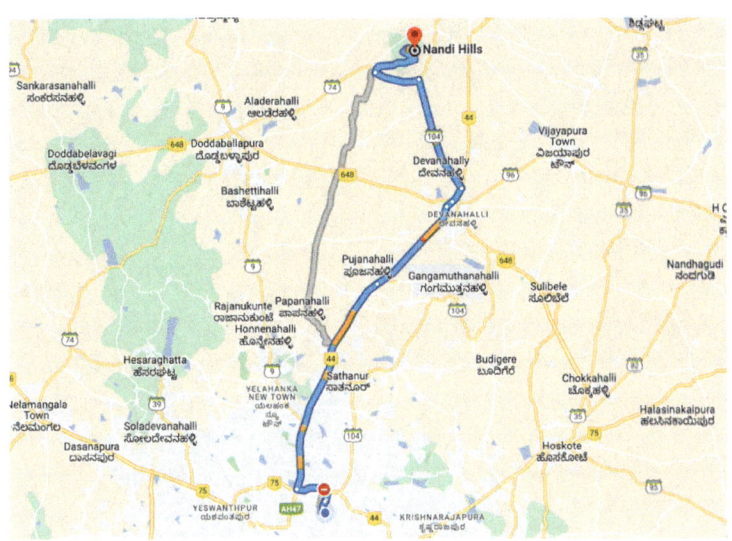

. 91. Road Map - Bengaluru to Nandi Hills.

111

About the Author

Partha Majumdar is just a programmer.

Partha has a passion for sharing knowledge. He documents his experiences in technical and management aspects in his blog: http://www.parthamajumdar.org. Also, he regularly publishes videos on his YouTube channel -

https://www.youtube.com/channel/UCbzrZ_aeyiYVo1WJKhlP5sQ. Partha has developed OLTP systems for Telcos, Hospitals, Tea Gardens, Factories, Travel Houses, Cricket tournaments, etc. Since 2012, Partha has been developing Data Products and intensively working on Machine Learning and Deep Learning. Partha has a panache for finding patterns in most of what he gets involved in. As a result, Partha has been helpful to teams in developing Rapid Development Tools.

Partha has continued to learn new domains and technology throughout his career. After graduating in Mathematics, Partha completed a master's in Telecommunications, a master's in Computer Security, and a master's in Information Technology. He has also completed two Executive MBAs in Information Systems and Business Analytics. He completed a PG Certificate program in AI/ML/DL from Manipal Academy of Higher Education (Dubai), an advanced certificate in Cyber Security from IIT (Kanpur), and a PG-level advanced certificate in Computational Data Sciences from IISc (Bengaluru). He is pursuing a Doctorate in Business Administration from the Swiss School of Business and Management (Geneva).

Books in this series

This book is part of a series named "Weekend Trips," which includes short trips to different parts of the world.

Weekend in Jordan

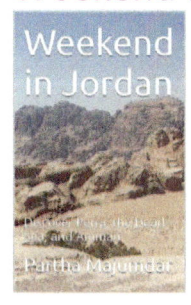

We planned a trip to Jordan to celebrate our 20th marriage anniversary. It was a last-minute plan, with tickets being purchased and bookings made just about a week before the travel. This was possible because Jordan provides visa-on-arrival for Indians. Jordan also provides visa-on-arrival for nationals of many countries. So, such a trip will be possible for many people worldwide.

The trip turned out to be quite an adventure for us. For a weekend, we felt like we were in a movie. That has etched the journey in our memories. Jordan is beautiful and is a wonderful country to explore. Being a relatively small country, exploring most of Jordan during the weekend is possible.

The book details our findings in Petra, the Dead Sea, and Amman.

Link in Amazon.com Store:
https://www.amazon.com/dp/B0CK5N6B3W

Elephant Ride in Chang Wangpo

Thailand welcomed ~11.5 million tourists in 2022. In 2020, tourism accounted for ~6% of the Thai GDP. We lived in Bangkok between 1996 and 1999. When another opportunity to visit Thailand came our way in 2018, we grabbed it.

Many things have changed in Thailand since our last stay. For example, traffic in Bangkok used to be a nightmare. On one occasion in 1996, I had waited at a traffic signal for ~45 minutes. Now, Bangkok has an efficient metro system, which has made getting to places very comfortable. Most of the good things we had enjoyed earlier are still in place. Getting to places outside Bangkok was never a challenge, as the road network is beautiful. This has only improved. The number of attractions has increased. And, of course, Thais are lovely people.

This was a business trip that overlapped with our 26th marriage anniversary. So, we decided to celebrate in Thailand while doing the needed business. During this trip, we revisited some places in Bangkok and Kanchanaburi. The surprise for us was the trip to Chang Wangpo, a once-in-a-lifetime experience.

Link in Amazon.com Store:
https://www.amazon.com/dp/B0CKGWH97S

Weekend in South Sikkim

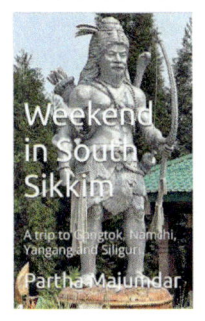

South Sikkim has several interesting places to visit. Generally, tourists to Sikkim explore places in North Sikkim like Gangtok, Nathu La Pass, Pelling, Yumthang Valley, etc. This book details what we found in South Sikkim.

We passed through Gangtok, Nathu La Pass, Tsomgo Lake, Baba Ka Mandir, Namchi, Char Dham, Samdruptse Monastery, Temi Tea Gardens, Yangang, and Bengal Safari in Siliguri (West Bengal).

Link in Amazon.com Store:
https://www.amazon.com/dp/B0CKL1DNTJ

Trips to Dubai

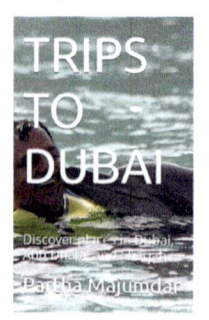

Dubai is one of the most visited tourist destinations in the world. Apart from beautiful places like the Burj Khalifa, Burj Al Arab, the Atlantis, and the Heritage Village, Dubai provides the opportunity to undertake thrilling activities. This book explores the different attractions in Dubai. Also, this book details activities, including the Helicopter ride over Dubai and playing with the Dolphins at the Atlantis.

The book also details attractions in Abu Dhabi and Sharjah, including the Ferrari World and Desert Safari.

This book contains my adventures in Dubai. These experiences provide details of nuances of traveling to Dubai and traveling within the Gulf region in general.

Link in Amazon.com Store:
https://www.amazon.com/dp/B0CKRYQKDN

Other Books by the Author

Learn Emotion Analysis with R

This book covers how to conduct Emotion Analysis based on Lexicons. Through a detailed code walkthrough, the book will explain how to develop Sentiment and Emotion Analysis systems from popular data sources, including WhatsApp, Twitter, etc.

The book starts with a discussion on R and Shiny programming, as these will lay the foundation for the system to be developed for Emotion Analysis. Then, the book discusses the essentials of Sentiment Analysis and Emotion Analysis. The book then proceeds to build Shiny applications for Emotion Analysis. The book rounds off by creating a tool for Emotion Analysis from the data obtained from Twitter and WhatsApp.

Emotion Analysis can also be performed using Machine Learning. However, this requires labeled data. This is a logical next step after reading this book.

Link in Amazon.com Store:
https://www.amazon.com/dp/B096K2SVF2

Linear Programming for Project Management Professionals

This book assists project management professionals in resolving project crashing situations as a linear programming problem. It demonstrates how the project management team can help streamline the project's on-time completion and cost optimization.

The book begins with understanding of project management processes and frameworks such as WBS, PDM, and EVM. The book helps familiarize the project management team with monitoring procedures. It helps investigate linear programming problems (LPPs) and the mathematical foundations for their formulation. It covers various approaches to solving the LPP, including graphical methods, their limitations, and the necessity of tools such as Microsoft Excel's Solver. It also covers how the project management team can solve LPP with the help of Solver.

This book covers various business and technical scenarios for crashing a project. It discusses how to formulate the problem of optimizing a project for time and cost as a linear programming problem. This book then discusses how linear programming problems can be solved using Solver and more complex issues. It also explores the relationship between earned value management and crashing a project.

Link in Amazon.com Store:
https://www.amazon.com/dp/B09PD1GFMY

Mastering Classification Algorithms for Machine Learning

Classification algorithms are essential in machine learning as they allow us to predict the class or category of input by considering its features. These algorithms significantly impact multiple applications like spam filtering, sentiment analysis, image recognition, and fraud detection.

The book starts with an introduction to problem-solving in machine learning and subsequently focuses on classification problems. It then explores the Naïve Bayes algorithm, a probabilistic method widely used in industrial applications. The application of the Bayes Theorem and underlying assumptions in developing the Naïve Bayes algorithm for classification is also covered. Moving forward, the book focuses on the Logistic Regression algorithm, exploring the sigmoid function and its significance in binary classification. The book covers Decision Trees and discusses the Gini Factor, Entropy, and their use in splitting trees and generating decision leaves. The Random Forest algorithm, a cutting-edge technology for classification, is thoroughly explained. The book rounds off with a detailed discussion of Boosting techniques.

Link in Amazon.com Store:
https://www.amazon.com/dp/935551851X

Corporate Lessons I Learned

In 34 years of corporate life as of 2023, many incidents have left a lasting impression on me. These lessons have helped me take up the upcoming challenges as I progressed. There have been so many people I have met. From each interaction, I found so many things to learn.

This book presents some of these interactions. While these incidents give hilarious recollections, they provide an understanding of the corporate world. As I have primarily been in middle management, this book provides a guideline for middle and lower-level managers for dealing with everyday challenges.

Link in Amazon.com Store:
https://www.amazon.com/dp/B0CL3YBSF8

Gartner Research Analysis

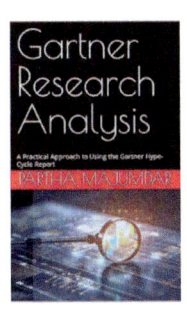

Gartner Hype-Cycle Report has a lot of information about new Inventions and Innovations. Apart from the details of the inventions and innovations, it also states the companies working on these technologies and their stage in getting their products ready for commercialization. It can be overwhelming to go through the details of this report.

This book systematically states a mechanism for using the Gartner Hype-Cycle report to draw valuable inferences. The mechanism is explained through a live case study. It shows how to narrow down the provided options for a given objective. Any such research will only be complete with a detailed analysis of the narrowed-down options by studying more material outside the report. The illustrated mechanism can be used as a precursor for using the Gartner Hype-Cycle report.

Link in Amazon.com Store:
https://www.amazon.com/dp/B0CK582Y2M

Creating an Investment Portfolio

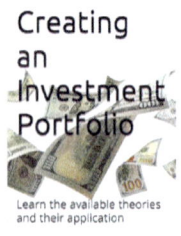

Investing is an essential requirement whether one is an individual or a corporation. If the right investment decisions are made, it can be fulfilling for the investor. Making the right decisions in investment is a scientific process. So, it is essential to understand the involved theories and their applications.

This book discusses portfolio creation's essential theories and applications, including fixed deposits, mutual funds, and shares. The discussion includes the needed mathematics. Also, simple and omnipresent tools that can be used for the calculations are illustrated.

This book will be helpful for both individual investors and companies.

Link in Amazon.com Store:
https://www.amazon.com/dp/B0CK99SPKZ

Printed in Great Britain
by Amazon